How You Became You shows the danger of two extremes of parenting—*rigid parenting* that leads children to feel trapped by parents' rules and expectations, with little sense of freedom; and *chaotic parenting* that leaves children no sense of belonging or guidance. The book then describes healthy parenting, where both structure and freedom are provided for children. I highly recommend it for parents who are trying to guide their children as well as for professionals who work with families, such as clergy, family life educators, and counselors.

Rev. Dr. Lanny Law, LMFT
Author of *God Knows Marriage Isn't Always Easy*

This book is about more than raising healthy children. It is also about being a healthy adult. Each of us has been affected by rigid and chaotic parenting directly or indirectly, within family or outside of it. *How You Became You* helps good parents become smarter parents, while equipping every reader with the basis of understanding that is necessary to truly be an agent of restoration in God's world.

Scott and Janice VanderKooy
Worldwide Christian Schools

How You Became You helps identif_ ___ __ ___ __ _ve upbringings and how they deeply affec_ ___ __ ___ as adults. The book takes the author's skill and exp__ience as a therapist and encapsulates her discovery of how two abusive parenting styles—rigid and chaotic—typically characterize the painful childhood experiences shared by her clients. The book reveals that one's efforts at self-improvement in adulthood are hampered by learned negative responses in part caused by the lack of a healthy upbringing. As the product of healthy parenting alternating with an unhealthy chaotic one due to parental mental illness, I strongly appreciate how the book helps me identify who I am in light of my upbringing, as well as what I can do to better myself as a Christian and parent.

As a pastor, I highly recommend this book to my fellow under-shepherds as a helpful resource to assist their congregations in identifying and overcoming their childhood development obstacles on the road to spiritual renewal and growth.

Rev. Harrison Newhouse
Hancock Christian Reformed Church
Hancock, MN

How You Became You (And Why You Do the Things You Do)

How Abusive Parenting Styles Debilitate Children

Judy R. De Wit

iUniverse, Inc.
Bloomington

How You Became You (And Why You Do the Things You Do)
How Abusive Parenting Styles Debilitate Children

iUniverse books may be ordered through booksellers or by contacting:

iUniverse
1663 Liberty Drive
Bloomington, IN 47403
www.iuniverse.com
1-800-Authors (1-800-288-4677)

Because of the dynamic nature of the Internet, any web addresses or links contained in this book may have changed since publication and may no longer be valid. The views expressed in this work are solely those of the author and do not necessarily reflect the views of the publisher, and the publisher hereby disclaims any responsibility for them.

Any people depicted in stock imagery provided by Thinkstock are models, and such images are being used for illustrative purposes only.

Certain stock imagery © Thinkstock.

ISBN: 978-1-4759-2677-4 (sc)
ISBN: 978-1-4759-2678-1 (e)
ISBN: 978-1-4759-2679-8 (dj)

Printed in the United States of America

iUniverse rev. date: 6/18/2012

Contents

Acknowledgments   vii
Note from the Author   ix
Introduction   xi

Part 1   Rigid Parenting Style   **1**
Chapter 1   Growing Up under Rigid Parenting   3
Chapter 2   What the Rigid Parenting Approach Looks
            Like   7
Chapter 3   The Effects of Rigid Parenting   15
Chapter 4   Stories of Rigid Parenting Approach   25

Part 2   Chaotic Parenting Style   **31**
Chapter 5   Growing Up under Chaotic Parenting   33
Chapter 6   What the Chaotic Parenting Approach
            Looks Like   37
Chapter 7   The Effects of Chaotic Parenting   43
Chapter 8   Stories of Chaotic Parenting Approach   51

Part 3   Healthy Parenting Style   **57**
Chapter 9   Growing Up with Healthy Parenting   59
Chapter 10 What the Healthy Parenting Approach
            Looks Like   61
Chapter 11 The Effects of Healthy Parenting   71
Chapter 12 Stories of Healthy Parenting Approach   81

Conclusion   **87**
Chapter 13 How You Became You   89
References   95

Acknowledgments

Special thanks to all my clients who were willing to share stories of their difficult childhoods, which enabled me to put together a continuum that can help them and others understand why they do the things they do and how they have become who they are today.

Because I love God above all, I thank Him for enabling and empowering me to write this book so that individuals and families can be touched and healed when they come to know who they are and why they do the things they do.

Judy R. De Wit

Note from the Author

After years of listening to clients tell their stories of childhood hurt and pain, I realized that typically one of two things was happening: Either they were telling me that their parents were rigid or harsh with them, or they were telling me that their parents never cared about them or what they did.

As time went along, I saw a pattern in how these clients were affected by the kinds of childhoods they had. Anxiety, perfectionism, obsessive-compulsive disorder (OCD), defensiveness, and reactivity were typical characteristics of rigid parenting. Promiscuity, poor boundaries, drug and alcohol abuse, codependency, and identity issues were experienced by those who had chaotic parenting.

I am convinced that essential to recovery from unhealthy parenting is first discovering what kind of parenting you experienced, how that approach internally affected you, and how that effect causes you to be who you are today.

A helpful question to ask is, "How did I become me and why do I do the things I do?"

Judy R. De Wit

Introduction

"Why didn't someone tell me this before?" is a question my clients frequently ask when I explain to them the two extremes in parenting approaches.

Whether you have participated in therapy or not, your inner self wrestles with the question of how you became who you are today. There's a longing within you to know why you do the things you do and how you got to be the way you are. One way to find some answers is to look at what kind of parenting you had as a child.

This book provides a discussion of two extreme parenting styles. One extreme is harsh and rigid parenting, and the other extreme is chaotic parenting. This book will help you to remember—or discover—what your growing-up years were like.

Once you uncover what kind of parenting style you were subjected to, the book will explain what typical characteristics you may exhibit because of it. As you begin to understand how you got to be you, you are free to choose what changes you want to make.

Read this book with your guard down. Be willing to admit that your childhood wasn't as great as you thought it was. Then come to the realization that your childhood greatly affected how you have turned out and be willing to search for what changes you need to make so that you can be the healthy person you desire to be.

Judy R. De Wit

PART 1
RIGID PARENTING STYLE

Chapter 1
Growing Up under Rigid Parenting

Honor your father and your mother.

–Eph. 6:2

She was depressed and anxious and was now in tears.

Confronted by her therapist to speak the truth, Lou[1] fell silent. All along she had struggled inside about whether to tell her therapist her real thoughts and feelings about her parents and her growing-up years. She had never told others or admitted to herself what those years were about because she was taught that speaking badly about her parents was disrespectful to them. Until now.

There were many rules. There were rules about her dress, rules about her behavior, rules about how to behave, rules about respecting authority, and rules about what to say and not say. There were rules about what she could and couldn't do on Sunday, rules about obeying her Sunday school teacher, and rules about what God wanted little girls to be like. There were rules about cleaning her room, doing the dishes, and how best

1 No real names are used for the examples in this book.

3

to vacuum the living room. She was expected to clean out the garage on Saturday, help her dad with the lawn in the summer, and babysit her sister when her mom and dad were gone. Sadly, all she could remember was that there were a lot of rules.

Her dad and mom were strict. There were punishments and scoldings when she didn't do as she was told. She remembered having to stay in her room for the day because she forgot to feed the dog. Another time her dad made her rewash all the dishes because one of them wasn't clean enough. Once when her bed wasn't made up right, her mom removed the bed from her room for the night. She slept on the floor instead.

There were punishments. She and her brothers were beaten and hit with a stick or a belt. She had bruises on her legs and her brothers had bruises on their arms. She feared that if her dad became angry, he would throw something at her. If she was bad, she knew that if her mom reported to her dad what had happened, things would be even worse when he got home.

She remembered her parents calling her names—like *stupid*, *lazy*, and *moron*. If she did something wrong, her mom would tell her grandma and then her grandpa and grandma would also discipline her and make fun of her for what she'd done.

Then there was school. Lou's parents expected As. Lou said that if she got a B on her report card, she was grounded for a week. She worked hard at learning how to play the clarinet, but her dad and mom said it wasn't good enough. She remembered giving a speech for a speech contest. Later, her dad made fun of her and told her that she shouldn't ever give speeches again. She went to her room and cried. A short time later, Lou's dad came into her bedroom and told her to stop crying like a baby.

When she was old enough to date, her boyfriends were never good enough for her dad. He was critical of them and said they were dumb and worthless. Lou and her dad often ended up fighting over the boys she dated. As time went along, Lou learned how to work around her dad. She did late-night sneak-outs or said she was going over to a friend's house when her dad asked where she was going. She was tired of his rules and was determined to do the things she wanted to do.

Lou was pregnant at age seventeen. Her dad and mom were furious when she told them. Hurt by the way they responded, she left to live with her boyfriend. She managed to balance having a baby and going to school. Eventually she married the child's father.

Things were never good enough for Lou's parents. It was never right. However hard she tried to be perfect, it wasn't good enough. And her parents made sure Lou knew that.

As she finished up the session, her face was wet with tears. For the first time in her life, she was honest with herself. She felt like a burden was lifted, and she realized how much her past had hurt her. When exiting the room, she turned to her therapist and said, "I cannot honor my father and my mother without first being honest with God and myself about what my childhood was like."

Chapter 2
What the Rigid Parenting
Approach Looks Like

Fathers, do not embitter your children.

–Col. 3:21

What is rigid parenting?

Rigid parenting is a parenting style that is driven by excessive rules and the use of anger to control and belittle children. Parents who practice this style of parenting demand perfection from their children, send messages that they don't measure up, and use high levels of criticism.

What does rigid parenting look like?

"It's never good enough." That is what rigid parenting is based on. Characteristics of rigid parents include

- blame;
- shame;
- guilt;
- anger;

7

- undermining decisions;
- narrow expectations/rigid boundaries;
- telling children how to think and feel;
- criticizing appearances;
- conditional love;
- threats;
- possessiveness and jealousy of children;
- the "know-it-all" syndrome;
- withholding acceptance and approval;
- creating a false self;
- physical and emotional abuse.

Let's take a closer look at rigid parenting.

Blame

Controlling parents blame. They blame their children or anyone else that is nearby for things that go wrong, even when it's not their fault. In the context of the family, these parents use statements such as "You weren't thinking," "You should have," "You never," and "You always." Children receiving the blame for things they didn't do come to believe it is their fault. And then they come to believe they are the problem.

Shame

When parents shame their children, they give messages to the children that they are bad, will never measure up, and aren't good enough. Through words and body language, they communicate to their children that they are lesser, defective, and will never amount to anything.

Shame is directed at the personhood of a child—not at what the child does. An example of shame would be when a parent tells their children that they are "stupid at math." Calling a child stupid is saying to the child that he or she is bad, doesn't measure up, and will never amount to anything. It's an attack on the child's personhood. Van Vonderen (1989, p. 41) defines this sort of shame as messages given to family members that they are defective and inadequate. He says that over time, these messages become ingrained into the family member and drive him or her to find ways to prove he or she is good enough.

Guilt

Rigid parents use guilt to control their children. Guilt messages are when parents use "should have" or "could have" messages about what the child did. "You never help your grandma with the dishes" is a guilt statement. Phrases like "You could have studied longer for that test," used when the child already spent significant time on the material, are designed to produce guilt. "You read too much. You should burn those books" is an example of a guilt message.

Anger

Rigid parents exercise unhealthy control over their children, dictating to them what to do and what not to do. They refuse to give their children choices, and they bark out orders when things need to get done. They control using anger, yelling, name-calling, and the silent treatment so their kids do what they're told. Physical punishment is frequently used when kids misbehave.

Undermining decisions

Rigid parents undermine the decisions of their children. If a child decides to buy a new outfit, his or her parents say that he or she paid too much for it. If a child signs up for a class at school, the child's parents say it'll never work. If a child finds a job to earn a little money, rigid parents will find some problem with it. Rarely, if ever, is the decision right, according to rigid parents.

Narrow expectations

Rigid parents have a narrow definition of how things should be. They have rigid boundaries, making others' viewpoints and opinions unacceptable; their way of doing things is the only way. This causes children's emotions to be restricted because their thoughts, feelings, and perspectives are diminished and squelched. According to Laaser (2004, pp. 94–95), when there is rigidity in families, abuse occurs when the rigid boundaries are used in such a way that children are not affirmed, loved, or encouraged. This leads to feelings of emotional abandonment.

Telling children how to think and feel

Rigid parents tell their children how to think and feel. They tell them they shouldn't be mad, they shouldn't cry, or they shouldn't be sad. When tears surface, they shame their children into thinking they are babies for crying, they have to learn to suck it up and move on, and they should quit making such a big deal out of whatever is bothering them. They feel sad or hurt, but Dad says to forget about it. They cry because friends won't play with them, but their parents tell them to straighten up. Their dog dies and they miss it very much, but their parents say they are babies for crying.

Laaser (2004, p. 97) says that family abuse happens when adults tell their children that their feelings are bad. He calls this a kind of "mind rape." He stresses the importance of allowing feelings to be felt so that issues, such as grief over the loss of a loved one, can happen.

Appearances

Rigid parents are concerned about how they look to others. They insist that their children behave in certain ways in public so they will look good. This means they want their children to dress right, say the right things, and comply with what others expect of them. Rigid parents get upset when their children share ideas that are different from the norm or express opposing positions on issues. It's an outright embarrassment if their teens get pregnant when not married, drink too much and get caught, or are arrested for shoplifting.

Conditional love

Rigid parents use conditional love. Conditional love is love that has to be earned. It is based on conditions. Children have to do certain things to earn the parents' love. It could be getting all As in school, doing certain chores around the house, or acting or behaving a certain way. However, rigid parents, because their love is conditional, withhold that love because whatever the children do is never good enough. They always find something wrong. For the children, this creates a tireless cycle of trying to get approval, but never getting it.

Threats

Rigid parents use threats to get their children to comply with their demands. These threats are unreasonable and confusing. They may threaten that the children will get no food for the day if they don't get better grades, or they'll have to live at the shelter if they don't behave. They may say things like, "The next time you show me an attitude, you're going to be locked in the garage."

Possessiveness and jealousy of children

Rigid parents are jealous parents. They get jealous when their children spend time with their friends. They want their children to stay at home with them, to stop calling or seeing their friends, and to be home to serve their parents. This possessiveness increases as children get older. Rigid parents want the attention of their children.

The "know-it-all" syndrome

Rigid parents are the "know-it-alls." They think they know everything on nearly every subject. Whether they actually read a book on a subject doesn't matter. How and what they think on an issue is what's right. They are the authorities on how to raise their own kids, how to raise other people's kids, and how to address issues at church. They are opinionated and narrow minded. Their know-it-all attitude prevents them from being teachable or from seeing another point of view.

Withholding acceptance and approval

Rigid parents want their kids to be perfect. Although the kids strive toward that expectation, they are never able to reach it. They are unable to reach it because whatever is done, it's never good enough. Because it isn't right or good enough, rigid parents withhold acceptance and approval from their children. Rigid parents do not compliment their children, affirm them, encourage them, or embrace them. They withhold approval because they lack resources within themselves to give it. They fear that complimenting their children will cause pride. They would rather take the chance of emotionally neglecting their children by not affirming or encouraging them than have to worry about them turning out to be proud.

Creating a false self

Children of rigid parenting are told what to do, how to think, and how to be. Opinions and self-expression are not allowed. Only what the parents think and feel has validity. Children are taught to keep their thoughts to themselves. What counts is what Dad and Mom think.

Physical and emotional abuse

Physical and emotional abuse typically accompany rigid parenting. Physical abuse can include excessive spankings, beating, and whippings. Rigid parents leave visible marks on their children, including bruises and welts. Physical abuse also leaves emotional marks on the children's hearts, creating fear, confusion, and loneliness. When physical abuse is used, the anger of the parents escalates to a point that it is out of control; it is more about the parents' insecurities and issues than about bad children. Rigid parents claim they use this kind of punishment because it was what their parents did to them, so it must be right and good. Physically abused family members fear for their physical safety (Laaser, 2004, p. 100).

Emotional abuse involves using words, body language, and any other communication style that belittles, shames, ridicules, and makes fun of another. In the context of rigid parenting, it is done to control the children. This control is unhealthy because it attacks and harms the personhood of the child. The child's very being is being destroyed instead of enhanced and encouraged. Children come to believe the shameful messages their parents give them. They then perceive themselves as worthless and hopeless.

Summary

Rigid parenting takes many forms. It includes using blame, shame, and guilt to control children. Rigid parents use anger in the form of yelling, name-calling, and silent treatments to force their children to comply with their demands. They undermine their children's ability to make decisions and tell them how to think and feel. Looking good to others is important and children have to earn their love. Rigid parents use threats and jealousy with their children, and they position themselves as the authorities in all things. They withhold acceptance and approval of their children. Rigid parenting can include emotional and physical abuse.

Chapter 3
The Effects of Rigid Parenting

Or they will become discouraged.

–Col. 3:21

Anxiety

The overall effect of rigid parenting is anxiety. The children of rigid parents are anxious because of the excessive criticism, anger, demands, and control their parents used on them. They fear they will make a mistake, they fear they will be ridiculed and shamed by their parents when they do, and they worry about whether or not things are perfect. Anxiety dominates the lives of children who grow up with rigid parents.

Rigid parents themselves are an anxious people. They have the same anxiety issues as the children they are raising. They fear mistakes, they fear that things aren't perfect, and they feel worthless when they mess up.

But the drive to be perfect isn't all there is. Along with it, children of rigid parents are driven to have others accept and approve of them in a way that Mom and Dad never could. They may look to their supervisors, co-workers, friends, and church members to see if they are good enough and measure up. They excel at nearly everything and are seen as overachievers—all in the hope that someone will validate them as good enough.

How rigid parenting affects children

Effects of rigid parenting include

- feeling blame for nearly everything;
- feelings of shame and guilt;
- feelings of anger;
- loss of self-confidence;
- tendency to think and feel as they're told;
- OCD tendencies and worries about appearances;
- acceptance and approval issues;
- being defensive and reactive;
- possessiveness and jealousy;
- fears of doing something differently;
- becoming either overly compliant or rebellious;
- developing a false self;
- experiencing physical or emotional abuse.

Let's take a closer look.

Feeling blamed for nearly everything

When children are blamed for everything, typically two things can happen when they reach adulthood. Either the adult children will fight back when blamed again, or they will continue to believe that it really is their fault and they can't do anything right. The fighting back is done out of exhaustion at being hurt so many times. Taking the blame without a fight is how they have learned to carry a chip on their shoulder and take on the role of victim.

Shame and guilt

Rigid parents' use of shame causes children to hate themselves. Shame causes children to view themselves as defective, useless, and bad. They come to believe that they deserve their punishments and the bad treatment their parents subject them to. They believe they don't deserve to be treated with respect.

Because of this, as soon as they speak up and share a thought or an opinion, guilt floods their souls. They think that someone who is as worthless as they are should not be expressing opinions and creating trouble, so they feel excessive guilt for expressing an opinion or a viewpoint.

Anger

Obedience is based on fear with rigid parenting. When Dad and Mom are angry, their children fear that they will be hit, shamed, ridiculed, and punished. This causes the children to withdraw, isolate, and shut down. They hide in their bedrooms and don't want to talk about things. They become scarce around the house in hopes of avoiding their angry parents.

Two things can happen when children are treated this way. One thing is that the children bury their hurt way down in their hearts and try to ignore it. This stuffing of their anger eventually creates stomachaches, headaches, and sleepless nights. They continue to try to do everything perfectly so there are no more blowups. They internalize their fear of their parents' anger and strive to keep their parents happy.

Secondly, the children take out their built-up anger on others. They may have anger fits at school, with friends, with siblings, and with themselves. They may bang their heads, talk about wanting to die, or find ways to stay at friends' houses. They mimic their parents' displays of anger and are not taught a healthy way to deal with their anger.

Along with anger, children of rigid parents learn that they need to lie to survive. They lie about where they were, how things happened, or what someone said. This is done not so much out of defiance as to survive rigid parenting. Children of rigid parents learn that lying is better because telling the truth may cause another anger explosion by the parents.

Loss of self-confidence

Rigid parenting undermines children's decisions, causing children to lose confidence in themselves. They come to believe they really can't make decisions and know what is best. Children lose trust in themselves when they need to make decisions, and they turn to their parents for help instead. This causes children to be dependent instead of independent.

Tendency to think and feel as they're told

As these children grow up, rigid parents tell them how to think and feel. Children aren't allowed to have their own thoughts or feelings. They become like puppets with strings: they just think and feel what they are told. Their feelings get suppressed deep down, and they begin to feel confused. They feel sad or hurt, but Dad says to forget about it. They cry because friends won't play with them, but parents tell them to straighten up. Their dog dies and they miss it, but their parents say they are babies for crying. Being told that their feelings are wrong or what they think doesn't matter creates confused children.

OCD tendencies and worries about appearances

Children of rigid parents become obsessed about many things. Obsessive Compulsive Disorder (OCD) is when there is repeated ruminating of the same thoughts or the repeating of certain behaviors or both. Children learn from their parents that they have to do things perfectly. This causes them to check and recheck and then check again to make sure that what they did is perfect. They worry if their bed was made right, if they washed the dishes perfectly, or if their clothes are wrinkle free.

Their obsessive thinking causes thoughts that keep on spinning. They obsess over whether they unplugged their curling iron, if they spelled all the words right in an assignment, or if they said something they should apologize for. This thinking often interferes with getting other things done.

Acceptance and approval issues

Rigid parents never tell their children they love them. They think that children should just know it, so there's no need to say it. As the children grow up, they yearn to hear that they are loved by their parents. Because it never comes, they start to do things in hopes that their parents will notice and then say they are loved. But it never happens.

But they do not give up easily. Knowing they are loved is central to their survival. So they continue to find ways to get love from their parents. They hope the way they do things will get them some love words. They hope that by being a certain way, they will hear how they are loved. They hope that if they achieve good grades and blue ribbons, or if they are good at sports, their parents will notice and affirm them. It never happens.

Children turn to others in hopes of finding love because they are driven by the need to be loved. At the workplace, they work extra hard, hoping to be loved and accepted. In relationships, they give a lot of gifts and do many kind things to try to "earn" love. They are driven by wanting to hear that they are loved.

Being defensive and reactive

Children of rigid parents easily feel threatened, which makes them defensive and reactive. They are easily threatened because of the many years they have been criticized by their parents. Whether they are guilty of doing something or not, their guard is up because they fear the criticism that may be coming. Their anger surfaces quickly and their replies are curt and sharp. They are out to protect themselves from any attacks. Children of rigid parents are defensive and reactive.

Possessiveness and jealousy

Rigid parents are jealous about the time their children spend with others. They want all of the attention. They want their children home with them. This possessiveness and jealousy causes children to feel guilty for being with friends. They can't enjoy time with others because they know that Dad and Mom want them home. When they are home, however, Dad and Mom are busy with other things and don't spend time with them.

Fears of doing something differently

Children of rigid parents fear behaving in a way that is different from their parents' way. Their parents taught them that their way is the one right way. Therefore, when the children have new or different ideas about how something could be done, the children are faced with guilt that they are not complying with their parents' wishes. This can also cause a great deal of anxiety.

Becoming either overly compliant or rebellious

In response to the "know-it-all" syndrome, children typically exhibit one of two traits. They either become overly compliant, or they rebel. To be overly compliant means that whatever is supposed to be done, whatever they are told to do, whatever is asked of them, they comply completely. They don't believe in expressing their own thoughts or feelings about an issue. They don't argue or debate issues; they simply obey. If Dad and Mom tell them that they need to look for a different job, they do it. If they are told to go back to school, they do it. If they are told to discipline their children a certain way, they do it. It's like they are unable to think for themselves. They are unable to know their own thoughts and feelings about things.

The opposite can also be true. Adult children of rigid parents can be rebellious. By the time they are in their late teens and early twenties, they are exhausted by all of the control and seek out to do the opposite of what they are told. They feel disrespected when Dad and Mom continue to dictate to them about their lives. When told to go back to school, they work at a low-paying job instead. When told to get their car fixed, they run the car till it dies. If told to send their kids to a Christian school, they'll send them to a public school. They drink till they're drunk, behave promiscuously, use drugs, sneak out at night, and are truant.

Developing a false self

Growing up under rigid parents makes children have false selves. This means that they don't know their own thoughts and feelings, but only what Dad and Mom would think about something. They become what Dad and Mom want them to be. Living as a false self is exhausting. And after a while, the exhaustion turns to anger because the adult children feel that they have no control over their lives.

Experiencing physical or emotional abuse

Rigid parenting is often physically abusive. This use of excessive physical punishment creates a child with anger issues. The child internalizes anger for being punished in this way and will either turn that anger inward or take it out on others. The child acts out the anger by hitting, biting, or kicking because he or she is unable to manage the anger appropriately. The child gets in trouble in school and then, in turn, gets in more trouble at home. Excessive physical punishments lower the self-esteem of the child, create self-doubt, and cause shame issues—all of which are not easily corrected. They can also lead to other symptoms, such as sleepless nights, excessive crying, mood swings, stomachaches and headaches, and separation anxiety.

Rigid parents are emotionally abusive. When the parents use a belittling and degrading approach toward a child, the child loses self-confidence and a sense of self-worth. The child easily takes the blame when things go wrong, believes that other kids don't like him or her, and either withdraws or rebels. This child spends excessive time alone or on the computer, doesn't want to play with friends, and doesn't share things with the family. The child could also become angry and explosive. Anger takes over because these children believe that they have little value or self-worth and that nothing can go right. Venting and raging occur, and their anger is targeted at themselves and others.

Laaser (2004, pp. 96–98) discusses three ways invasive emotional abuse occurs in families. The first way is when children are outwardly told they are bad, won't amount to anything, and should never have been born. The second way is when children are told that their feelings are bad. They shouldn't think like that, they shouldn't feel that way, and they should be mad about that. The third invasive emotional abuse approach is when a parent has a bad marriage and uses a child as a companion, buddy, or friend. This is called covert emotional incest (p. 98). When this happens, the child no longer has his or her own thoughts and feelings. The parent and the child have a relationship like that of a married couple. The child learns to do and think as the parent wants. The child neglects his or her own needs and emotions because the parent has stolen them. Eventually this leads the child to have identity issues.

Summary

When rigid parents use shame, blame, and guilt on their children, the children grow up with fears of being bad people, feel guilty easily, and fear sharing their own thoughts and opinions. Parents' use of anger and discouragement give the children large amounts of anxiety about how to do things and make decisions. Children of rigid parents struggle with knowing their own thoughts and feelings. They obsess about doing things perfectly and worry what others will think of them. The parents' use of conditional love teaches their children that love is not free—it is earned. Children of rigid parents are defensive and reactive. They know that their parents are jealous of their attention, and they believe that their parents always know best. As children of rigid parents come to their teens and early twenties, they either rebel against all of their parents' rules or learn to over-comply to all of their demands. These children grow up striving to be the person their parents want them to be, living as a false version of themselves. Rigid parents are often emotionally and physically abusive to their children.

Chapter 4
Stories of Rigid Parenting Approach

A violent man leads one down a path that is not good.
—Prov. 16:29

Myra

Myra said that work was difficult. She explained that while at work, she felt anxious and at times had to go home for the day. She was frustrated with this because she didn't know why it was happening and couldn't figure out what she was anxious about. Usually her problems with anxiety happened at work, but lately, she was feeling anxious at the store and at home.

She had gone to the doctor the week before. She told the doctor that sometimes her heart pounded hard and her chest got tight; a few times she thought she was having a heart attack. After running tests, the doctor found nothing wrong with her heart. He suspected that she was experiencing panic attacks and he recommended therapy.

As she sat in the counselor's office, she said she couldn't understand what could be wrong. Describing her childhood as normal and good, she said her dad had high expectations and goals for her. Because of her good grades, her dad wanted her to be a doctor. Although she really didn't want to go to medical school, she agreed, since her dad said that he would help pay for some of the costs.

She said that her mom kept a house cleaner than anyone she knew. She remembered how when she was young, her mom never allowed her to have toys or games out, she had to clean and straighten her room before leaving for school, and her friends weren't allowed to come over for a play date because they would mess up the house.

She was a good student. Her parents expected As, and she got them. For every A on her report card, she would get five dollars. When she got anything lower than an A, her parents would be upset with her. There was one time she got a B+ in one of her classes. Not only was there no money but also she was grounded for a week. She pressured herself to make sure she got only As after that.

She was in many school activities and programs. She excelled at playing the violin, played several school sports, and was involved in a writing club. She told how she helped out with church activities, participated in volunteer groups for the homeless and poor, and liked to participate in the community theater whenever she could.

With that, she stopped.

"It is never enough. The things I did were never good enough for my parents. No matter how hard I tried, there was always something wrong with the things I did. Even now, when I buy something, there is always something wrong with it. It's too big, the color isn't right, I should have waited for a sale, or they tell me I don't need it."

Then it occurred to her. She was beginning to see how she was seeking her parents' approval for things. She realized that whenever she did something, she turned to her parents to ask if it is good enough or if it was what she should do. She felt like she was unable to think for herself or make her own decisions. It was as if they had power over her.

As she thought about these things, she began to realize something: she needed to do her own thinking, feeling, and decision-making. She knew she had to stop asking for her parents' approval and be satisfied with her own decisions. The power they had over her—by commenting on her performance and her decisions—had to end. She wanted to embrace her own thoughts and feelings and decisions and stop looking to her parents to make sure it was okay.

As she reflected, she shared more. "I think I do the same thing at work. I look for my supervisor's approval and acceptance, and I want my co-workers to like me. I know I do good work. But at the same time, I am asking those around me if it is good enough. I guess that comes from my childhood." Her therapist agreed.

After several weeks, the anxiety began to lessen. As she learned how to accept herself and what she did, her fears diminished. The undermining that her parents had done to her was changed to self-affirming thoughts. Her need to be involved in so many activities to try to prove her worthiness decreased. She became more casual and relaxed, and her need for perfection lessened. She was taking pressure off herself to perform a certain way, and she was starting to like herself the way she was.

Several months later, she realized something else: she was laughing more. She learned not to take herself so seriously, making mistakes was a part of life, and having tried is better than not having tried at all. She was on the road to recovery.

Sam

His father believed in a lot of physical punishments. Beatings, whippings, and spankings were common during his growing-up years. Sam and his older sister would often have bruise marks on their bottoms and legs, and withholding food was a common punishment.

With his eyes filled with tears, he explained that his dad had unreasonable and unnecessary rules. If he did something one way, his dad would tell him it was wrong and he should have done it another way. If he did it that way, then his dad would say that wasn't right either.

When asked if the school ever reported anything about the bruises, he said yes, but back then, when social services became involved, they often sided with the parents. Child protection didn't do anything to protect kids.

Sam said that his dad never showed emotion. His dad never told him once that he loved him or that he cared about him. Sam's dad never hugged him, or for that matter, praised him. Sam's mom was around, but she was scared of Sam's dad. She made sure that she stayed out of his way when he became angry. Sam described his mom as a wimp and said that she enabled his dad to treat the kids the way he did.

Sam's dad believed that his way was always right. It didn't matter what happened; he was sure he knew best how to handle the situation and dictated how it was supposed to be done. He was that way at church and in the community. He often argued with the preacher, thought he knew more than the doctor, and threw things when people didn't do as he said. His favorite phrase was, "That's the way it's always been done."

Sam shared that his dad had also touched his sister inappropriately. With all of his rules, one wouldn't think he would do such a thing. But it was as if his dad thought he had the right to do what he wanted, and so he did. Sam's sister told him about the times he would do things when their mom had gone to work night shifts. He would come into her bedroom and touch her. His sister never told anyone but him.

Sam's boss had fired him the week before he started counseling. He believed he couldn't do anything right anymore, even his job of twelve years. He didn't think anything was worth trying, and he wanted to stay in bed and sleep. He took responsibility for losing the job because he had assaulted a co-worker.

His anger was out of control, his depression was severe, and his self-esteem was nearly non-existent. His challenge was to make changes that would build him up to be the person God intended him to be.

Charles

He described himself as rebellious. Charles said that from the time he could remember, he never wanted to listen to anything his dad or mom told him. To him, it seemed that they had too many rules. He described his parents' parenting approach as similar to treating children like birds locked up in a cage.

From the time he was very little, he could remember all of the rules his parents had. And he hated every one of them. When they spelled out a rule, his first thought was how to break it. Of course when he did, he was punished. Dad liked to spank and Mom liked to yell and shake her finger at him. It was exhausting.

His parents did not believe in giving him choices. He had to wear what they said to wear, take the classes they thought he should take, and only have the friends they approved of. He felt controlled and diminished by them and started to hate everyone.

By the time Charles was a teen, he was done with his parents and anyone in authority. He was in trouble at school and was arrested for vandalism. He was charged with driving under the influence. He eventually got a girl pregnant.

The reality of what he did began to sink in. Being in trouble with the law was difficult and the thought of being a father scared him. He turned to his therapist and said, "Why did I do all of this? Why am I so angry?"

Charles was able to answer his own questions. He told the therapist that his parents never really listened to him. In fact, he didn't think they knew him or what he was about. Because they were always worried about all of their rules, they never spent time with him. They never encouraged or praised him, and they never shared with him what they saw as his gifts and strengths. He said that no matter what he did, it was never good enough. It was never right. Their overcorrecting approach drove him to rebel and to hate everything about them. He admitted that he put up his own walls against them. If they weren't going to listen to him, he wasn't going to listen to them either.

His parents' approach to parenting left him feeling disrespected and belittled. Their control, strict discipline, and punishments made him feel disempowered. This made him rebel. By breaking the rules and fighting back against their authority, he hoped that he could gain power in a powerless position. It didn't work. His challenges for therapy will be to work through his fears of being controlled, to be less defensive and reactive when confronted, and to use corrective thinking when he berates himself for doing things the wrong way.

PART 2
CHAOTIC PARENTING STYLE

Chapter 5
Growing Up under Chaotic Parenting

You have had five husbands, and the man you have now is not your husband.

–John 3:18

She laughed.

Then she turned to her therapist and said, "My parents never cared about what I did or where I went. I would leave for days at a time. They never went to look for me or call around to see where I was. I didn't matter to them. It made no difference if I showed up at home or school or at grandma's house. As long as I came around within three days, it was good enough for them."

Tears surfaced.

Then Faye added, "They were always at the bar. I remember when I was little, my little brother and I would wait in the car for hours while my dad and mom were in the bar drinking. Sometimes we would get so tired of waiting for them that we would walk home instead, which was about two miles. When my brother and I got home, I would put us both to bed. Usually past midnight, I would hear Dad and Mom come home. They were often drunk and would stagger around the house until Dad collapsed on the floor. I can still see Mom opening my bedroom door to make sure I was in bed. It was awful."

Faye continued to talk about her crazy childhood. When asked what kinds of rules her parents had, she couldn't think of any. She couldn't recall any mealtimes together, any sort of discipline used, or how she ever made it to school in the mornings. She knows that she went to school because she remembered which teachers she liked and which ones she didn't. School was a good experience for her. She believes she liked it because it was the place where adults—the teachers—cared about her.

Her house never had food. She could remember feeling hungry. Her mom never had money, and the cupboards and the fridge were always empty. There was a small drugstore near her house. She remembered that at the age of five she would go into that store and steal food. She said she would try to take enough for her and her brother. Shoplifting became a part of her life. She needed food, and that was one way to get it.

When she was about ten years old, Faye's parents divorced. Prior to that, there was a lot of yelling and arguing, so when her mom told her they were moving out, Faye wasn't surprised.

But there were new problems at the house they moved to. The problem was her mom's boyfriends. And her mom had a lot of them. It seemed that she took home a new boyfriend every few months. Although she couldn't recall much about them, she remembered one of them by the name of Mark.

At first Mark was fun. He often brought over food and treats for Faye and her brother. He would play games with them and sometimes took them out to eat French fries. However, as time went along, things with Mark became different. One time, he came into Faye's bedroom and touched her in a bad way. Another time, he showed Faye pictures of naked people. There was also one time when he made Faye sit down and watch a movie of two people having sex together.

Faye became silent. Tears fell as she re-experienced the hurt and loneliness of those years. It seemed so confusing. It seemed so surreal. It was so scary.

She reflected. "I have so many questions," she said. "I have questions about why this happened and about where my mom was when he did this to me. I want to know why no one ever stopped him and why the police weren't called."

After she gathered her things to leave the room, she paused to touch a book that was on the shelf. She looked at the title of it and then smiled and said, "You have a book about forgiving your parents. That is something I need to think about. Do I need to forgive my parents? One would think that parents would know what it means to be a parent. But that's not true. I think that some parents are only kids themselves, looking only to satisfy their own needs."

Chapter 6
What the Chaotic Parenting Approach Looks Like

Sin is lawlessness.

–1 John 3:4

What is chaotic parenting?

Chaotic parenting is a parenting approach characterized by few to no expectations, or rules, and little structure for the parents or their children. The parents' lives are driven by satisfying themselves with whatever feels good at the moment.

What does chaotic parenting look like?

Chaotic parenting is drenched in a "whatever" attitude.

Chaotic parenting is characterized by a lack of structure. There are little to no rules about what children should and shouldn't do. Children learn to fend for themselves, having to do such things as finding food to eat, getting to school, doing their homework, and helping their younger siblings get the things they need.

Chaotic parents typically have addictions. Drugs, alcohol, gambling, and other addictions dominate their lives. Establishing a life with structure and purpose becomes even more difficult because of these addictions. They seldom manage to get up in the morning and get to work. They don't expect themselves to accomplish things around the house. Typically, they do not know where to begin and do not have enough energy or self-discipline to achieve goals, so failure is almost a foregone conclusion.

Chaotic parents and the children raised by them seldom know who they are. Because they do not know who they are and what they can do, they stumble through life striving to belong.

Characteristics of chaotic parenting include

- no rules;
- no structure;
- no expectations;
- chaos;
- codependency;
- poor boundaries;
- permissiveness;
- addictions;
- false self;
- sexual abuse.

Let's look more closely.

No rules

Chaotic parents do not believe in rules for themselves or their children. They approach issues and life with a "whatever" attitude. They believe that life just happens, and they respond to it as it happens. They view rules as bothersome, especially since rules interfere with the enjoyment of life. Following rules is a lot of work, and they prefer not to work.

They view having rules for themselves as bad because the rules would mean they would have to do something. If they had rules for their children, that would be bad because they would have to hold their children accountable for what they were doing. Accountability is work, and chaotic parents don't like to work.

No structure

Chaotic parents do not use structure. Structure, such as expecting kids to get up at a certain time, having them get ready for school, and making sure they get to bed on time for the next day, is difficult for chaotic parents. Even structuring and accomplishing something themselves is difficult. When given the directive to accomplish three or four things by supper time, chaotic parents become overwhelmed.

No expectations

Chaotic parents don't have expectations for their children. They don't expect children to do as they're told or do chores around the house. Because they don't have expectations for themselves, they rarely expect anything from their children. This is how their parents did it, and this is how they do it.

Chaos

Life is confusing when there are no rules, structure, or expectations. Life for the kids of chaotic parents means not having clean clothes to wear, not having food for lunch, and not having their health care needs met. Some chaotic parents do not care where their children are. When their children don't come home at night, they don't bother finding out where they are. It doesn't matter. When they show up, they show up.

Parents who have chaotic homes do not attend to the emotional needs of their children. They do not attend to issues of their children being hurt or wronged by another. They believe that somehow things will work out.

Codependency

Chaotic parents are often codependent with multiple sexual relationships. They typically have been married more than once, have had sex with others while married, and don't believe in settling down with one person. They approach relationships as easy come, easy go.

It's not unusual for women to have six or seven children from four or five fathers. And it's not unusual for fathers to have six or seven children with that many different women. Chaotic parents believe that having kids is a result of having sex with each other. They don't believe in getting married first, having sex, and then having children.

Poor boundaries

Boundaries are where a person says yes or no to those around them. With chaotic parenting, there are poor boundaries. This means that the parents approach relationships with an attitude of doing whatever they want to each other. Chaotic parents exhibit poor boundaries when they spread gossip and slander about their children, or show disrespect to their children or put them down, privately and publicly. They may allow their children to watch movies and other media that are inappropriate.

Poor boundaries for these parents include the parents sexually abusing their children. Molesting, fondling, and sexual intercourse may occur with chaotic parents. They think sexually touching their children is okay because chaotic parents don't use boundaries. They live by the idea "Do as you want. It's a free world."

Permissiveness

Chaotic parents are permissive. This means that when issues surface, they don't take up the slack. There are no rules about dating or curfew, and whether or not children go to school is their own decision. If the school reports that their child is disruptive, they tell the school to handle it; it's their problem. Or they will tell the school that what the child did isn't that bad. "It could be a lot worse," is the parent's reply.

Addictions

Chaotic parenting often accompanies parents who have addictions. These addictions can be drug and alcohol, pornography and other sexual addictions, gambling, shopping, or something else. These parents have little to no expectations for themselves, so drinking till they get drunk or going to the bar every night is okay. If someone addresses the addiction issue to the chaotic parent, the warning is ignored. The chaotic parent is defensive about being able to do whatever he or she wants to do.

False self

False self happens when children manipulate others to get things to go their way. They want to belong to someone because Dad and Mom have not left them with a secure sense of belonging. They rescue and over-function in hopes of being loved by someone.

Sexual abuse

Few rules and boundaries exist in the chaotic family. This causes a lack of protection for family members because they are allowed to do what they want with each other. Therefore, in chaotic families, sexual abuse is often found. Inappropriate touching, fondling, and intercourse can happen when chaotic parenting is used because there is no respect for one another.

Summary

Chaotic parenting is about the parents' failure to use rules or structure for their children. They have no expectations for their children or themselves. Things at home are chaotic. These parents believe that having sex with multiple partners is okay, and they are negligent in establishing and using appropriate boundaries. They use a permissive approach to parenting their children. This approach is a "whatever" attitude that they use for themselves and for their children. Addictions occur and a false self develops. Sexual abuse can occur when there's chaotic parenting.

Chapter 7
The Effects of Chaotic Parenting

A fool finds pleasure in evil conduct.
                                                    −Prov. 10:23

Who am I?

The largest effect of chaotic parenting is the inability of the children to know who they are. They never come to know who they are, what they are good at, or what their strengths are because of their lack of structure and expectations. In their struggle to know who they are, they often become codependent and have many sexual relationships because they are trying to find their identities in other people.

They may also have difficulty managing emotions because of their childhood experience. This difficulty of managing emotions can come from childhood sexual abuse and neglect and abandonment issues. They have learned to manipulate others as a way to survive.

Children of chaotic parents grow up to be codependent. They are unable to determine who they really are, so they hook themselves up with others in search of an identity. This identity is drenched with over-functioning to get others to like them, becoming what they think others want them to be, and exhibiting chameleon-like characteristics in their hopes of getting someone to like them and accept them.

Also, in their search of who they are, chaotic parents have multiple sexual relationships. They marry and divorce many times, use sex to get others to love them, and have several children from many different partners. Drugs and alcohol addictions are typically a part of chaotic parenting and often the addictions of the parents become the addiction of their children.

The ways chaotic parenting affects children include

- obedience is not learned;
- unpredictable family life is experienced;
- expectations are not learned;
- a lack of teaching accountability and responsibility;
- codependency is learned;
- poor boundaries are used;
- permissiveness is allowed;
- addictions occur;
- a false self develops;
- sexual abuse can happen.

Let's take a closer look.

Obedience is not learned

When children have no rules, they never learn to obey. When they don't learn to obey, they have no respect for authority. This causes children to have an attitude that they don't have to listen to their parents or other adults because "they can't make me."

When there are no rules, children are scared. Their world is scary because without rules, there is no one to protect them when bullies wrong them. They know they are an easy target for harm and ridicule when others say or do things to them.

Children who grow up without rules can grow up without a conscience. They do not learn about right and wrong because no one showed or told them. They come to believe that they can do whatever they want, and that if they do wrong to another, it's fine. It doesn't really matter if they hurt someone.

When children aren't taught to obey rules at home, they also believe they don't have to listen to rules at school or in their community. These children often are truants, shoplifters, or liars, and frequently get in trouble with the law.

Unpredictable family life

Life is confusing when there is no structure for children. Getting up at a certain time, getting ready for school in a certain way, and having supper at the same time nearly every evening creates predictability and safety. They come to know when things are done, how they are done, and what comes next. When there is no structure, these things don't happen. Therefore, life for these children is chaotic.

Children without structure are anxious. They become anxious because they don't understand what may happen next. Unpredictable family life means that children do not know if or when Mom is coming home, whether they as a family will eat supper that evening, or if Dad and Mom will be at the bar for the rest of the night.

Expectations are not learned

Parents must expect their children to do certain things. Parents expect their children to tell the truth, help out with household chores, be kind to others, and respect adults and others.

Chaotic parents do not approach life that way. For them, it doesn't matter if their children lie, have temper tantrums, break things, or miss school. They don't expect their children to behave a certain way. Therefore, when their children don't do something, it doesn't matter because there are no expectations.

When parents don't expect things from their children, children don't learn to expect things from themselves. There is little to no self-discipline. Grades don't matter, dressing appropriately doesn't matter, and what kind of language they use makes no difference. Whether or not the children attend school regularly, how much they lie and cheat, or if they excel in sports or other school activities, children of chaotic parents come to believe it doesn't matter.

A lack of teaching accountability and responsibility

When the home is chaotic, so is the child. Children who live in chaos are unable to structure their own lives. At school, they can't find their pencils, don't know where their homework is, cannot focus on getting things done, and typically cry because of their frustrations.

Chaotic parents neglect the needs of the child. These unmet needs include emotional needs, physical needs, and intellectual needs. When a home is chaotic, so are the ones who come from that home.

Accountability and responsibility are lacking in the child who comes from the chaotic home. The parents of this kind of home are negligent about getting their bills paid, buying groceries, managing money, and staying employed. They struggle with knowing what to do first, how to solve problems, and how to treat their spouses and families.

Codependency is learned

Children of chaotic parents are often promiscuous and codependent. Having sex at an early age is likely because chaotic parents do not teach their children to set and use boundaries. Often in a search for who they are and who they belong to, hooking themselves up sexually with others gives the momentary hope that they belong to someone. This codependency and promiscuous behavior are not about building relationships with others. Issues of trust, honesty, and compatibility are not a part of this kind of relationship. Rather it is about seeking out someone to belong to and being temporarily loved by someone.

Chaotic parents have multiple sexual relationships. They often marry several times, have several affairs, and try to belong to someone by offering sex. These parents often have many children, partly because of their own recklessness in controlling pregnancy, but more out of their belief that having children will mean someone loves them.

Poor boundaries are used

Chaotic homes have poor boundaries, causing the chaotic parenting approach to be invasive and intrusive. Because of this, sexual abuse is often found in chaotic homes. Chaotic parents don't believe in respecting the boundaries of others. They believe they can do what they want to others, and they use conning and manipulation to get their children to comply with their demands.

Laaser (2004) speaks about the use of loose boundaries within family relationships. He describes the boundary as an invisible area where others intrude and invade family members' territory. This loose approach is about people who don't have control over themselves and invade the private territory of others. Loose boundaries should not be used in the family context.

Because the home environment is chaotic, children don't know what to do when they are being abused. Often they will try to minimize it and hope that it won't happen again. They are confused about what is happening to them when they are being sexually abused, but they fear telling someone about it.

Permissiveness is allowed

When parents are permissive, so are their children. Permissiveness in this context means participating and supporting things that most know are wrong or harmful. It is permissive when children are allowed to talk back to authority, engage in sex before marriage, and use vulgar language. It is permissive when parents allow children to make decisions that are the parents' responsibility, such as when they may start drinking or dating. Parents who hand out birth control to their teen because they fear the teen will become pregnant are permissive.

Addictions occur

When parents are chaotic, the children often have addiction issues. They turn to drugs, drinking, sex, shopping, poker, and other addictions because they want to escape from their chaotic lives. As they enter adulthood, their addictions continue and can worsen. Now because they fear structure, such as going to work and supporting themselves and a family, they are overwhelmed and they turn to their addictions to escape responsibility and accountability.

False self

Their false self is pretending to be someone they're not so that they will be loved and accepted. They become what they think others want them to be. After a time, this becomes exhausting, and they are unable to continue. This also creates anger about what they are doing, and that anger gives them the energy to stop pretending.

Sexual abuse can occur

Sexual abuse happens in chaotic families because there are poor boundaries, no rules, no expectations, and little respect for others. Children of chaotic families are especially vulnerable to predators because these children are not protected by their parents and because parents themselves neglect to be safe persons for their children. When victims of childhood sexual abuse become adults, they often suffer from abandonment and rejection issues, trauma, and post-traumatic stress disorder (PTSD), and have difficulty with managing their emotions.

Summary

When chaotic parents fail to have rules, structure, and expectations for their children, the world becomes a scary place. The children fear the unpredictability of their home lives and believe that nothing really matters. With such chaos, these children fail to learn and understand what accountability and responsibility are, what marriage and having one sex partner really means, and where and how to say "no" to others around them. Permissiveness dominates, leading to more confusion about what is right and wrong in their lives. Chaotic parents turn to addictions to manage stress in their lives, which eventually teaches their children to use addictions to escape life's difficulties. As children of chaotic parents yearn to belong to someone, they become whatever it takes to be loved and accepted by others. This pretending to be someone they're not is their false self. Sexual abuse often occurs when there is chaotic parenting because of the lack of protection of their children.

Chapter 8
Stories of Chaotic Parenting Approach

The wicked bring shame and disgrace.
−Prov. 13:5

Annie

Annie said that her dad was out of the picture. He left before she was born, and much of what she remembered about her youth was that she could do whatever she wanted. Her mom worked three jobs and was never home.

Because of this, she described her childhood as free. She was free to do was she wanted, including spending time with neighborhood friends, going to the mall when she wanted, and meeting up with some bad kids from school. It didn't matter when or if she got home in the evening because her mom wasn't there anyway. And when her mom did call to check on her, she managed to talk her way out of where she'd been and what she was doing, and her mom fell for it.

As she entered her early teens, she knew she was on her own. She admitted that she learned to be good at lying to her mom, she was able to steal from stores when she wanted something, and she came up with excuses when she missed school. Her mom was uninvolved with her school. When Annie's mom was home, she was so tired she spent most of her time sleeping, and her life was about being with friends.

During Annie's high school years, things worsened. She spent overnights with boyfriends, started using drugs and alcohol, and referred to herself as a gang member. It felt good that she belonged to someone (the gang), and having sex with boys she knew made her feel special and needed.

Annie's mom began having her own boyfriends at the house. Some of the men were from work and some were men she met at the bar. When Annie and her mom fought, Annie told her mom that she couldn't boss her around because she was doing the same things Annie was.

Now in her thirties, Annie was tired. She was tired of the chaos and confusion in her life. She was tired of pretending and faking it. She was tired of people taking advantage of her. She no longer knew who she was.

Annie's life and spirits were debilitated because both of the parents were absent from her life. With no adult supervision, she learned to survive on her own, which led her to solve her own problems with no accountability. By becoming what she thought others wanted her to be, she lost herself and had no boundaries. With no structure, rules, and expectations, she was on her own. This led to promiscuity, a lack of identity, and codependency.

Jerry

Jerry's dad was a drunk. He drank every day, and when he wasn't drinking, he was smoking pot. Sometimes he would go to the bar for the evening. Other times he would invite his friends over and they would hang out in the garage and drink till they were drunk.

When Jerry's dad drank, he became hostile and violent. Jerry described his dad as a yeller who would hit and throw things, and one time he remembers mom getting a black eye. Jerry's dad gave Jerry his first drink of beer when he was six. It happened again from time to time, and he learned to like beer by the time he was ten.

Jerry's mom was a pushover. Sometimes she would run into the bedroom when his dad was violent, and other times she would go to extremes to try to appease and calm him when he was in a bad mood. Some of Jerry's anger was directed at his mom for not doing what she was supposed to do to protect him.

Shortly after getting his driver's license, Jerry was cited for driving under the influence. While being held at the local jail, he called his dad and told him what happened. His dad arrived a short time later, paid the bail, and brought him home. Nothing else was said about the incident.

Now that he was in his mid-twenties, he realized his anger was out of control. He was charged with domestic violence, had assaulted a police officer, and child protection services had asked him questions about a report they received.

His life growing up was chaotic. With an alcoholic father and a weak mother, both of whom neglected to supervise and parent him, Jerry was left with no skills or tools to structure his adult life. What was normal for him was to turn to beer and violence in response to problems. He thought his chaotic childhood was normal.

Jessie

Jessie was sexually abused by the age of twelve. Being the youngest, with four older brothers, she was an easy target and was used and abused by them. After several incidents of assault, she told her parents what was going on. Her parents didn't believe her. They told her that she was lying and that her brothers would never do that to her. Nothing else was done.

Fearing it would happen again, she reported what was happening at home to her teacher, who became concerned. After the teacher spoke to the principal about what Jessie had said, the teacher told her that the police would be called.

Jessie was gripped with fear. She explained to them that if her parents found out that she reported it, things at home would get worse. She was told there wasn't a choice in the matter, and the authorities were called.

When an officer and a social worker contacted her parents and visited with them, the parents became indignant. The parents told them that their daughter was depressed and made things up. They said that she was an attention seeker and would do anything or say anything to get attention. When the officer and the social worker met with Jessie and asked her what happened, her story matched what she'd told the teacher. When they interviewed the brothers, they admitted they'd done what Jessie said.

Jessie was removed from the home and put into foster care. Her parents were charged with negligence and had to appear in court. The brothers were also charged and were required to complete a long list of court requirements. The brothers were eventually placed in a long-term residential treatment facility.

Jessie's parents used a chaotic approach to parenting. Refusing to believe her when she reported what was happening and neglecting to investigate or call the police to investigate the matter were sloppy and reckless approaches to a serious situation. Blaming Jessie by saying she was someone who sought attention diminished the importance of what needed attention. Their own denial about what their sons were doing was proof of their inability to respond properly to criminal activity.

PART 3
HEALTHY PARENTING STYLE

Chapter 9
Growing Up with Healthy Parenting

Train up a child in the way he should go.
—Prov. 22:6

Alyssa explained how she got drunk. She was at a party with one of her friends who knew college kids. At the party, some of the college kids were drinking beer, and she and her friends wanted to join in. She knew this was something she wasn't supposed to be doing, but she couldn't resist the fun.

Now she was facing three things: charges for driving under the influence, school violations, and dealing with her parents. She had been in trouble at home before, but never quite like this.

She said that when she called her parents to pick her up from the police station, they refused. They said that she chose not to obey the law and the repercussions were that she had to spend the night in jail. They would get her in the morning.

The next morning, Alyssa and her parents met with a police officer. They were told that a court date would be coming up for Alyssa and there were fines to be paid. The parents said they understood, took down the contact information, paid the money, and headed to school with Alyssa.

When they arrived at school, she and her parents went into the school building together. They headed for the school office and asked to meet with the principal. In that meeting, Alyssa's parents told the principal that Alyssa had something to report. She told her story. After a discussion among the four of them, Alyssa was sent to class, while her parents continued to meet with the principal to discuss what action the school would take, if any.

That evening, her parents confronted Alyssa about what she had done. They told her that she would be paying for the fines, would not be allowed to be with friends or go away for a month, and would be doing community service work instead. They told her that a certain amount of money from her part-time job would be used to pay off the fines, that she would be helping at the community food shelf and soup kitchen, and that she would be paying for the increase in their car insurance.

She said that she understood and would follow through on what they expected.

Several months later, in session, Alyssa explained that she was fulfilling all of the court requirements and what her parents were expecting her to do at home. Although in tears, she managed to acknowledge that she had it coming, but at the same time said she was angry that the consequences were excessive.

Her parents responded in healthy ways by holding Alyssa accountable for what she did and expecting her to be responsible for the damage and fines she had created and to give back to the community through community service projects.

Chapter 10
What the Healthy Parenting Approach Looks Like

*The wise heart is called discerning and pleasant words
promote instruction.*

–Prov. 16:21

What is healthy parenting?

Healthy parents use discipline and punishment in appropriate
ways, expect responsibility and accountability from their
children, and accept and love their children for who they are.

What does healthy parenting look like?

Healthy parenting is flexible.

Flexibility in healthy parenting searches and strives for the
middle of the road when dealing with children. Control is about
choices and expectations; accountability is about answering
to authority when rules are broken, and the use of guilt and
shame is centered on what a child does, not who the child is.
Responsibility is taught at an early age, love is unconditional,

and the children's own feelings and emotions are acceptable. Healthy parents teach their children how to problem solve and let them know that it's okay to make mistakes. Parents use appropriate boundaries and expectations for their children. Every family member is a contributing member to family and society. The belief that the world belongs to God is instilled in them at an early age.

Healthy parenting stresses a child's growth from dependence to independence. This means that the parents give tools and experiences to their children that enhance the development of their skills and abilities while giving them support and encouragement when things go wrong. Healthy parents do not let their children manipulate them, do not need acceptance and approval from their children, and can be okay when their child is miserable. They do not rescue children when they have made reckless decisions, they are able to control their own anger, and they can admit their mistakes and apologize when necessary.

Characteristics of healthy parenting include

- explaining choices and expectations;
- stressing accountability;
- appropriate use of guilt and shame;
- teaching responsibility;
- giving unconditional love;
- allowing feelings and emotions;
- solving problems and making mistakes;
- expecting children to contribute;
- enhancing skills and abilities;
- not allowing manipulation;
- not needing acceptance and approval;
- recognizing boundaries in parenting;
- controlling their anger;
- apologizing when necessary.

Let's look closer.

Explaining choices and expectations

Healthy parents give their children choices and let them experience the consequences of those choices. If a child chooses not to do his homework, the child is also choosing to be in trouble with the teacher the next day. If the child chooses to hit a sister, the child is also choosing to miss supper at the table. If the child chooses to throw popcorn on the living room floor out of anger, he or she is also choosing to vacuum it up and miss time with friends.

If the child tends to be strong-willed, using choices may help make the child more cooperative. An example is when a child needs to clean his or her room. The issue is not *if* he or she is going to clean it; the child is allowed to choose by when he or she is going to clean it. The parents could say, "Your room needs to be cleaned this Saturday by 4:00 p.m. If it's not done by then, you won't be going with us for pizza."

Expectations are what the parents expect from their children. Respect for each other, obeying their parents, and following through on what they are told to do are examples of expectations. Children do things because they know that is what Dad and Mom want. Children help Grandma with the dishes because that is what their parents would want them to do. Children put their games and toys away before bedtime because they know that is what Dad and Mom expect. They help button up their younger siblings' coats and help them with their boots because that is what Dad and Mom expect.

Stressing accountability

Accountability is about answering to each other. Teachers hold their children accountable for doing their homework, supervisors hold their workers accountable for being on time

Solving problems and making mistakes

Healthy parents know the importance of teaching children how to solve problems. Problem solving is not about the parents solving the problem for the child, but rather about helping the child to see the problem and explore the options for solving it. Healthy parents can give direction as to what should be done, but sometimes, letting the child choose the undesirable direction is a part of the learning process.

For example, a child is insistent that he can do his math homework without any help. The healthy parents know that how he is doing the assignment is not right. The parents encourage the child to do it differently, but the child doesn't want to listen. The child is insistent that "that is what the teacher said." Healthy parents are okay with backing off and letting the child find out later that it was done wrong.

Expecting children to contribute

Healthy parents teach their children that everyone in the family is a contributing member of that family. This means, no matter what the age, everyone can help out with something around the house. The child does his part, even if it is as simple as putting a dish in the dishwasher. Every member contributes to the family by carrying the groceries in from the car, picking up pieces from a game, or folding the laundry.

Enhancing skills and abilities

God created each person with skills and abilities. No matter what the age, no matter what the ability or disability, all family members offer their talents and gifts to their family, school, and community.

As healthy families know, skills and abilities range drastically from child to child. One may be good at music, one at sports, one at art, and one at making friends. Whatever the gift, healthy parents recognize early on the talents and gifts of each child and seek out ways to help their children become even better and more confident.

Not allowing manipulation

Children are good at manipulating. They are naturally selfish and egocentric, and healthy parents know this. Healthy parents don't budge when children seek out ways to work things so they go their way.

A teenage boy wants to go out with friends on the weekend. His parents have already said no because these particular friends are not a good influence on the teen. He is angry about their decision and throughout the week threatens to run away if he doesn't get to go. The parents remain unshakable and reply that should he run away, the police will be called.

For several nights in a row, a young girl tells her parents that her homework is finished and she wants to play video games. They agree as long as homework is finished. A call from the teacher a few days later says that several assignments are missing. The parents confront the child and find out that she was lying about homework. As the conversation continues, it becomes apparent that she also was neglecting chores around the house and instead conning her sister to do her work for money. The parents call the teacher the next day to say their child will be staying at school an extra hour each day until the work is caught up. The parents inform the child that the video game set will be sold.

Not needing acceptance and approval

Healthy parents know who they are and are well grounded in what they expect from their children. In the parenting role, they do not need the acceptance and approval of their children. They do not need to be adored, applauded, or stroked by their children. Healthy parents know the importance of staying in their role as parents and never becoming their children's friend. The self-esteem of the parents is healthy and strong.

When children disobey, healthy parents step in and discipline. And if the child does not like the discipline and the child's anger says that his parents are the meanest and worst parents ever, the parents remain unshakable. When the child expresses hatred for his or her parents and he or she wants to live somewhere else, the parents respond that it's okay that the child hates them, but they will always love him or her. If he or she wants to live somewhere else, they can discuss options of where to go.

Recognizing boundaries in parenting

Healthy parents use good boundaries and resist over-functioning. Over-functioning is about rescuing and doting over children. Healthy parents are not concerned about being a supermom or superdad. Healthy parents are focused on being a "good enough" dad and mom. A good enough dad and mom meet their children's physical, emotional, academic, and spiritual needs.

Healthy parents do not rescue their children. They believe in warning them, advising them, and directing them. But when children choose other than what was suggested, healthy parents let it happen.

Healthy parents do not worry about how much fun their children are having in church. Healthy parents do not rescue children who get in trouble with their teacher. Healthy parents are okay with an officer talking to their teen when he or she breaks the law.

Controlling their anger

Healthy parents know how to control their anger. Because of their own good self-awareness, healthy parents know what their triggers are, what to do when those triggers are triggered, and when to ask their spouses to take over when their anger escalates. Healthy parents know they must let their anger subside before dealing with their children and find ways to calm themselves so no damage is done.

VanVonderen (1992) writes about the importance of parents not squelching a child's feelings of anger, but instead giving the opportunity for the child to express that anger. The anger must be expressed appropriately, such as having the child say what he or she is angry about. Slamming doors or disrespectful comments should not be tolerated. He also cautions that just because the child is angry about what he or she was told to do does not mean the child doesn't have to do it.

Apologizing when necessary

Healthy parents know they are not perfect. Because of that, they know that when they make mistakes in their parenting, they should not be above apologizing to their children. Admitting that their temper was out of control, acknowledging that they failed to help when it was needed, or saying they are sorry because they forgot to do what was promised are examples of healthy parents knowing the importance of apologizing.

Summary

Healthy parenting is about giving choices and having expectations for children. This parenting style believes in holding children accountable for what they do and focusing on developing a good sense of guilt and shame in their children. Responsibility and unconditional love are used by healthy parents. They allow their children to feel and express their emotions without allowing their children to manipulate them. Providing opportunities for their children to problem solve and make decisions, teaching them that all family members contribute to family, school, and their community, and encouraging their children to develop their talents and abilities are what healthy parents do. Healthy parents do not need the acceptance and approval of their children and do not over-function in their role as parent. They are able to control their anger and believe that apologizing to their children is necessary when they have wronged them.

Chapter 11
The Effects of Healthy Parenting

Live lives worthy of God.

–1 Thess. 2:12

Healthy adults

The greatest effect healthy parenting has on children is that healthy parents create the greatest possibility that children will become healthy adults.

If children are given the opportunity to learn what it means to be responsible children, they will most likely be responsible adults. Having experienced what it means to be held accountable for actions and behavior, having been loved unconditionally, and having been provided the opportunities to identify and develop their skills and abilities, children become adults who are confident, self-sufficient, and self-reliant.

Self-esteem and self-confidence are strong when there was healthy parenting. Openness about feelings and emotions, knowing and accepting oneself, and being able to discern right from wrong increase the possibility of success, both in career and relationships. Seeing oneself as a contributor to family and community, dealing directly and honestly with people, and using healthy boundaries with others causes these adults to become flexible, high-functioning, and successful.

The ways healthy parenting affects children include

- teaching them about choices and expectations;
- teaching them to be accountable;
- giving them a healthy understanding of shame and guilt;
- teaching what it means to be responsible;
- helping them to understanding unconditional love;
- enabling them to deal with emotions;
- teaching how to problem solve and make decisions;
- showing that everyone is a contributing member of society;
- enhancing and developing skills and abilities;
- using honesty in relationships;
- teaching self-reliance and independence;
- keeping healthy boundaries;
- controlling anger;
- knowing when to apologize;
- enabling them to be their true selves;
- making abuse rare.

Let's take a closer look.

Teaching them about choices and expectations

Adult children of healthy parents make good choices. This does not mean they always make the right choice. It does mean they know how to approach decisions and choices by thinking through the possible consequences and repercussions of the decisions they make. They have developed the skill of making good choices because of many opportunities to practice while they were children and teens.

Growing up with healthy parenting means that all along parents had expectations for their children. The children learned that things were expected from them, whether those expectations were spoken or unspoken. When they became adults, they knew what was expected from them, such as paying bills, maintaining steady employment, working hard, and being honest.

Teaching them to be accountable

When healthy parents hold their children accountable, the children continue this behavior as adults. Now as adults they continue to be accountable to their spouses and families, church leaders, and communities. They answer to those around them and they hold others accountable to them. Accountability enhances integrity and honesty, two values that are core to healthy people.

Giving them a healthy understanding of shame and guilt

Guilt and shame taught by healthy parents help children understand right and wrong and help them experience guilt and remorse when they do wrong. Healthy parents know how to balance the amount of guilt and shame in their children so that when they come adulthood, they are better equipped to manage emotion and shame when they make mistakes again.

Negative self-talk does not occur because shame and guilt were not used excessively. Children of healthy parents know how to separate what they did wrong from who they are because of what they were taught about shame and guilt. So instead of beating themselves up when they did something wrong, they know that what they did was wrong, but they themselves are not bad.

Teaching what it means to be responsible

Because they were taught to do chores and complete tasks, adult children of healthy parents continue to be responsible. Instilled in them is the idea that if they commit to doing something, they will do it. They offer help when they see a need, they do things without being asked, and they live responsibly by following through and carrying through on what they say they will do.

Helping them to understand unconditional love

Unconditional love is when healthy parents love their children for who they are, not for what they do. Their children do not try to get others to love them by doing things for them. They don't see love as something to earn. They know that love is not about manipulating others. They do not fear or worry about rejection, isolation, or abandonment.

Because they are loved just for who they are, they have learned to love themselves just for who they are. They accept and embrace what they are good at and what they are not good at, they can laugh at themselves, and they are not easily hurt when wronged. Their love for self is not a selfish kind of love, but one that gives thanks to God for how they were made.

They are able to love others easily. They are equipped to more readily accept and love others because they know and understand themselves. They do not demand that others behave a certain way, are not overly critical, and want what is best for others. Their love is genuine.

Enabling them to deal with emotions

Growing up with healthy parents teaches children that it is okay to have feelings and express them appropriately. Healthy parents take the time to help their children understand their feelings, such as fear, happiness, sadness, and anger. Healthy parents do not squelch or make fun of kids when they cry easily or become sad. Instead, healthy parents help their children understand their feelings and help them to accept their feelings as part of who they are.

These children, with the help of their parents, have practiced understanding their feelings for many years. Because of this, when they become adults and adult issues surface, they can face those issues by using adult feelings. They can more readily separate their logical thinking from their feelings, they are able to accept the feelings of others as okay, and they are aware that feelings can become slippery and are not always trustworthy.

Teaching how to problem solve and make decisions

Problem-solving and decision-making issues are not a threat for children who grew up with healthy parenting. They learned early on that life is full of decisions that need to be made. They are aware that the outcomes of those decisions can be good or bad. They know that with God's help, most decisions can end in success and accomplishments.

When the child comes to an age where life decisions need to be made, such as college and career choices or marriage and family decisions, tools to make those decisions are in place. Again, this does not mean that their decisions turn out right every time. But it does mean that they have more resources within themselves to know how to proceed when problems arise and decisions need to be made.

Showing that everyone is a contributing member of society

Everyone helps out with problems and chores. Healthy parents teach early on that everyone is a contributing member of the family and society. This means that everyone has a task or chore to do, and the child is not to hold back and wait for someone else to do it. It is about being assertive, speaking up when something needs to be said, offering to help when there are needs, and being quicker to give than to take. Children of healthy parenting contribute to their families, churches, and society.

Enhancing and developing skills and abilities

While growing up with healthy parents, children learn what they are good at. Whatever it is, they do it and become it so God is glorified.

Adult children of healthy parenting are prepared for this stage of life because they know what they are good at. Their self-confidence is strong and they seek out new opportunities and learning curves because they are okay with succeeding and failing. These healthy adults are not proud or arrogant. They know their limitations, and use their influence to help others develop what they are good at.

Using honesty in relationship

Children of healthy parenting engage in relationships that are direct and honest. They do not need to work the system so that things go their way, they are open and honest about what they are thinking and feeling, and they express themselves in ways that enhance communication.

Teaching self-reliance and independence

Children of healthy parenting do not seek out others' acceptance and approval. They have confidence in what they do and how they do it, and therefore, they do not need to ask others if things are okay. They can determine when advice and direction are needed and know how to use the help to make an informed decision. They have little worries or concerns about whether people like them. They know they love themselves and they find their confidence in that.

Keeping healthy boundaries

Children of healthy parenting know about boundaries. They know it's important not to over-function when it comes to helping others, and they understand that rescuing others is not healthy. They allow others to fail and make mistakes, knowing that it's okay when things aren't perfect, and that children learn best when they face the consequences of their choices.

Controlling anger

Children of healthy parenting know about anger. They know the importance of managing their anger, what triggers their anger, and what techniques work when they need to calm their anger. They know that anger is not a bad thing and should never be about hurting themselves, others, or property. Talking about their feelings (including their anger) is something they do openly, and they are not embarrassed when their own emotions surface.

Knowing when to apologizing

Children of healthy parenting know the importance of apologizing. They realize that saying they are sorry for what they did brings healing to those harmed and can restore relationships. Owning the wrong is about acknowledging what they did, apologizing for it, and asking for forgiveness. These children know how and when to apologize because that's what they were taught by their parents.

Empowering them to be their true selves

When people know their own thoughts and feelings and can respond to the world around them in honest and direct ways, they can be their true selves. A true self does not become what Dad and Mom say they have to be or what their friends say they have to be. Instead, even when the pressure is great, they can think and do things that are best for them.

Smedes (1993, p. 153–155) speaks about the false self that comes from the unhealthy shame parents give their children. This false self speaks about how a person has to be in order to be acceptable in one's faith, culture, and family. Smedes asserts that with God's grace, the false self has no validity and shame has no threat. God's grace gives people the courage to face their fears of being rejected and the courage to know and believe that God accepts them.

Making abuse rare

It can't be said that healthy parents never abuse their children. However, because healthy parents have good self-awareness and control of themselves, it is rare. They do not believe in using harsh physical punishments or the shaming and degrading of children. They do not believe that children should be seen and not heard. They do not believe in provoking their children to anger or in being critical and harsh with them, and they do not have unreasonable expectations for them. They do not engaged in inappropriate touching of their children or others, and when they learn of other adults engaging in inappropriate activities with children, they report those adults to the authorities.

Healthy parents respect their children without giving them the control, allow children to express themselves without being manipulated, and know when to step away when they become overly frustrated. Healthy parents believe in logical and natural consequences, are invested and engaged in their children, and know their children are made in God's image.

Summary

Children of healthy parents become healthy well-adjusted people. They are skilled in decision-making, have expectations for themselves, and hold themselves and others accountable. They feel ashamed when they make mistakes, but know that those mistakes are things they did, not who they are. They take responsibility for what they need to do, and they love unconditionally. Feelings and emotions are openly expressed and they have good problem-solving skills. Their view is that everyone is a contributing member of their family and society, they know their talents and abilities, and they are honest in their dealings with others. They do not seek out acceptance and approval from others and can set and use boundaries appropriately. Being aware of their triggers, they know how to manage their anger and apologize when they have wronged another. They know who they are and embrace their true selves. They are not abusive to their children or others and have healthy boundaries in their relationships.

Chapter 12
Stories of Healthy Parenting Approach

The mind controlled by the Spirit is life and peace.
—Romans 8:6

Michael

Michael and his friends especially enjoyed the latest technology and technological equipment. They frequented technology stores, discussing with each other what was new and how the devices worked, and what they could do with them if they owned them.

Their biggest issue was money or the lack thereof. There was no way they could afford all the devices they wanted, and their parents weren't interested in helping out. Frustrated with the situation, they began thinking of what else they could do to get what they wanted.

Michael said that one evening the guys were over and they started discussing some of the new equipment their school had bought. They discussed what they liked about the video projector, what they could do with the big screen, and how they wished they had a computer system like school had. The more they talked about it, the more they wished they had it.

Then came the idea. Michael said he and his friends started daring each other to steal the school equipment. The more they talked, the more they were sure they could do it. Michael said that one of the guys' dads had a key to school. This friend had been with his dad several times and had watched him get into school in the evenings when everything was closed up. He knew there was a security system that needed to be shut off once they were inside and there was a master key that could get anyone into any room. Together they were sure they could do it.

Several weeks later, it was time to execute the plan. They needed to be on the school grounds at 10 p.m. One of them would come in a pick-up, another would have the needed keys, and Michael and two others would come with flashlights and hand tools. They were sure it would work.

But it didn't. The key worked and they were able to get into the building. But once inside, they were unable to shut off the alarm system. It was a matter of minutes before the police showed up at the door. They were caught.

The parents of the young men were called immediately. When they showed up, the police told them what happened and said that the boys would have to come to the police station for a report. The parents agreed to meet them there.

By the time they were finished at the police station, it was past midnight. His parents told him how angry they were about what he'd done, and they were going to support everything the officers said should happen. With court dates coming up, his parents told him that he would be grounded for the rest of the semester. They told him that they would be calling the school janitor and Michael would be required to do work around school for two hours every day for a month, and that a letter of apology would be written to the principal, the school board, and the school community and would be printed in the school newsletter.

The parents' approach was healthy because they showed full support for the legal system, they required their son to pay back the community he harmed, and their sin was made public by requiring Michael to write a letter to the principal, the board, and the school community.

Rebecca

Rebeccca's mom told the therapist that her daughter refused to get up in the morning and go to school. She was in the fourth grade and for several mornings had had angry outbursts and tantrums because she didn't want to go to school. This was making the mornings very difficult. Rebecca would throw things and break thing when she was told she needed to get ready for school. She said she was tired of being bossed around and felt that she didn't have to listen to anyone. She refused to change.

When Rebecca continued to be uncooperative, her parents stopped explaining and threatening and instead developed a plan.

The next morning, Rebecca again refused to go to school. She said that she was staying in bed and she wasn't going to listen to anyone. Although she was reminded several times to get ready for school, she didn't do anything. She stayed in bed.

When it came time for her to leave for school, her parents carried out their plan. They picked Rebecca out of bed and put her in the car, still in her pajamas with her hair uncombed. Rebecca and her parents headed to school.

Upon arriving at school, all three went into the building. Her mom said that by now Rebecca was crying, but her parents were unshakable. They went to the office and asked if they could speak with Rebecca's teacher. When the teacher came, they explained to her that Rebecca would be wearing her pajamas at school that day. The teacher was told that if Rebecca was uncooperative or defiant in any way, she should call and they would be back to address the issue. The teacher agreed.

Her mom said that as they were leaving, Rebecca was putting on her socks and shoes. She was trying to dry her tears and tie all of the buttons on her pajamas. With one last warning, her mom and dad left.

It was healthy for the parents to be directly involved with their daughter. They refused to let the child have control and they ignored her manipulation. They were able to show who had the power in the relationship and used discipline that fit the offense. The parents' involvement in this situation communicated to their daughter that they cared about her. There were rules, structure, and expectations, and the parents made sure they were carried out.

James

James was six years old and was not obeying his parents. His bad behavior was escalating, and his parents knew that he was getting out of control.

One evening James took a bag of popped popcorn and sprinkled it all over the living room floor. When his dad came upstairs and saw it, he was angry at what James had done. Firmly taking him by the arm, James's dad marched him to the closet where the vacuum was stored. Plugging it in and turning it on, he gave the power hose to James and told him that he was to vacuum until all of the popcorn was cleaned up.

At first, James thought this was fun and games. He pushed the vacuum fast and pretended that he was an actor on stage, doing dances with the vacuum. After about five minutes, James became tired of it. He told his dad that he didn't want to do it anymore. He wanted to quit.

But his dad was not buying it. He directed James to areas that needed more work and said it didn't matter if James was tired; he was going to vacuum until the mess was cleaned up.

After some time, James was in tears. He said that he was sorry for what he had done and he wouldn't do it again. With most of the popcorn picked up, James's dad said that he could shut off the vacuum, but he wasn't done yet. James was directed to remove the vacuum cleaner bag, carry it to the garbage, and find a new bag to replace it. With some help from his dad, he did it.

Seating him on a chair in the dining room, James's dad directed him to write a letter of apology to both his parents for disobeying them and for making a mess in the living room.

When apologies were accepted and hugs were given to assure James that the incident was over, his parents reminded him that their love for him is unconditional.

Healthy parents strive to use punishments that fit the offense. They make sure they hold their children accountable for what they did, carry through on punishment, and assure their children that the issue is over when apologies are made.

CONCLUSION

Chapter 13
How You Became You

(And Why You Do the Things You Do)

You, be strong in the grace that is in Christ Jesus.
−2 Tim. 2:1

We have walked through a discussion of two extreme parenting styles and explored a third. If we were to draw out what this book describes on a continuum, it may look something like this:

Rigid   Healthy   Chaotic

X_____ X_____X

Here are some questions to consider:

1. What kind of parenting style did your dad and mom use on you?
2. Where on this line would you put yourself and why?

3. What kind of parenting style did your spouse's parents use on your spouse?
4. Where on the line would you put your spouse and why?
5. What drives you?
6. Why do you do the things you do?

With these questions in mind, read the descriptions of different kinds of persons listed below. See if you can determine what parenting style was used.

Description:

You are an anxious person. You worry about whether you are good enough at your job, you ask people if what you buy is okay, and you seek out the approval of others. You worry about everything and fear that people don't like you. You tend to overapologize and become stressed when you think you may have said something unkind to someone.

> *Parenting style:*
> It's likely that one of your parents was rigid and controlling. Your parents never affirmed you, never said they loved you, and did not approve of what you did. You seek to be approved and accepted by others today because you didn't get it when you grew up.

Description:

You are a perfectionist. You fear criticism, and when it comes from your supervisor, you fear that you will be fired. You believe your value comes from not making mistakes, and when you do, you beat yourself up and believe you are a failure.

> *Parenting style:*
> It's likely that one of your parents was rigid and controlling. As you grew up, you strove to be perfect

because you knew if you made a mistake, you would be punished and humiliated. Fearing the shame and ridicule from your parents, you learned early on never to make a mistake because making mistakes is bad.

Description:

You can never find your papers, get to an appointment on time, or know what you are supposed to do. Your house is a mess, your bills are never paid on time, and your spouse is frustrated by your approach.

> *Parenting style:*
> It's likely that one of your parents was chaotic. You create the same chaos they did. When you were a child, they didn't have expectations for you or hold you accountable for the things you did, and you grew up thinking that chaos was normal.

Description:

Your teen is pregnant. As you think about that, you realize that you also had sex by age fourteen, that you were promiscuous throughout high school and college, and that your dad and mom never cared about what you did or where you were.

> *Parenting style:*
> It's likely that one of your parents was chaotic. With few to no boundaries, with no rules and guidelines for what is appropriate behavior, you started engaging in sexual activity as a teen. Saying "no" was never taught, and the cycle from parent to child repeats itself.

Description:

Your teen is pregnant. You and she have been fighting for the last two years. She says that you are too strict and harsh. You say she is bad and doesn't listen. She is angry. You are angry.

> *Parenting style:*
> It's likely that one of your parents was rigid and controlling. You also became a rigid parent, which in turn caused your daughter to rebel and go against your control by becoming pregnant.

Description:

You are defensive and reactive toward others. When someone suggests something to you, your feelings are hurt. You have a quick response to their "criticism" and you defend yourself, even though you know the suggestion was good.

> *Parenting style:*
> It's likely your parents were rigid and controlling. You are not receptive to new ideas or suggestions because it feels like your parents' criticism all over again.

Description:

You look for others to love you. You are willing to become what someone else wants you to be and allow others to control you. You want to belong to a group, even if the company is bad. You enable them to use you and even abuse you because being loved by someone abusive is better than not being loved at all.

> *Parenting style:*
> It's likely your parents were chaotic. You saw your parents become what others told them to be, all in the hopes of being accepted and loved. Your dad abused your mom, and your mom took it. They pretended they were someone they weren't.

Description:

You don't know who you are. You aren't sure what your talents and abilities are because your parents never told you. You feel insecure when you try things. You lack confidence and good self-esteem because you have identity issues.

> *Parenting style;*
> It's likely your parents were chaotic. They were so confused about what they were supposed to be doing that they didn't structure a home life for you, leaving you to fend for yourself. Because your parents didn't tell you what they saw in you, you are left wondering what you're good at.

Description:

You fear change. You believe that your way is the right way and other ways are wrong. Whether it's at home, at church, or in the community, you become angry and upset when others want to do something differently.

> *Parenting style:*
> It's likely your parents were rigid. While growing up with rigid parents, you were taught that it was their way or the highway. You now take that same approach toward other adults. In fact, you think you know it all and others don't know what they're talking about.

Conclusion

By discovering what kind of parenting style you had, you will be able to develop an understanding of how you became you and why you do the things you do.

Should you find yourself on either end of the continuum, know that the goal is to be in the center of the continuum, where healthy parenting is found. If you are on the rigid end, you need to lighten up on all the rules and harshness and let grace and love filter in. If you are on the chaotic end, you need to structure your life, hold yourself accountable and responsible to those around you, and increase the expectations you have for yourself and others.

The center of the continuum is the place where you learn to balance your life. No one ever happens to be there; instead, one must work at being in a healthy place. Your rules, expectations, responsibilities, and relationships need balance. Using a give-and-take approach, doing things in moderation, having good self-awareness, and flexing and bending are all about healthy parenting.

Be willing to search for who you are and how you became who you are today. Once you know, challenge yourself to make changes so that you are all God intended you to be.

References

Laaser, M. *Healing the Wounds of Sexual Addiction*. Grand Rapids: Zondervan, 2004.

Smedes, L. *Shame and Grace*. San Francisco: HarperSan Francisco, 1993.

VanVonderen, J. *Tired of Trying to Measure Up*. Minneapolis: Bethany House Publishers, 1989.

VanVonderen, J. *Families Where Grace is in Place*. Minneapolis: Bethany House Publishers, 1992.